F SAINT LAWRENCE • GULF OF MAINE • B

• NARRAGANSETT BAY • LONG ISLAND SOUND • NEW YORK

• CARIBBEAN SEA • GULF OF GONÂVE • GULF OF HONDURAS

LF OF DARIEN • ARGENTINE SEA • NORWEGIAN SEA • NORTH

BOTHNIA • CENTRAL BALTIC SEA • GULF OF RIGA • ØRESUND

EA • BAY OF BISCAY • CANTABRIAN SEA • MEDITERRANEAN

N SEA • ALBORAN SEA • BALEARIC SEA • GULF OF SIDRA •

SEA OF SARDINIA • SEA OF SICILY • TYRRHENIAN SEA • SEA

• DENMARK STRAIT • ARCTIC OCEAN • CHUKCHI SEA • EAST

CHORA SEA • WHITE SEA • WANDEL SEA • GREENLAND SEA •

SEA • AMUNDSEN GULF • HUDSON STRAIT • HUDSON BAY •

SEA • BASS STRAIT • BELLINGSHAUSEN SEA • COOPERATION

DRAKE PASSAGE • GREAT AUSTRALIAN BIGHT • GULF SAINT

A • RIISER-LARSEN SEA • ROSS SEA • SCOTIA SEA • SOMOV

MAN SEA • ARABIAN SEA • BAY OF BENGAL • GULF OF ADEN

PERSIAN GULF • RED SEA • TIMOR SEA • PACIFIC OCEAN •

CK SEA • BO HAI • BOHOL SEA • CAMOTES SEA • CELLEBES

SEA • EAST CHINA SEA • FLORES SEA • GULF OF ALASKA •

LAND • HALMAHERA SEA • JAVA SEA • KORO SEA • MAR DE

J SEA • SEA OF JAPAN • SEA OF OKHOTSK • INLAND SEA •

TASMAN SEA • VISAYAN SEA • YELLOW SEA • SARGASSO SEA

OCEAN

OCEAN

A VISUAL MISCELLANY

BY **RICARDO HENRIQUES** AND **ANDRÉ LETRIA**

chronicle books · san francisco

Dedicated to all sailors, even those who just wet
their fingers before turning a page.—R. H.

To my grandmother Madalena and to Joana—A. L.

First hardcover edition published in the United States of America in 2018 by Chronicle Books LLC.
Originally published in Portugal in 2012 by Pato Lógico Edições, Lda.
Text copyright © 2012 by Ricardo Henriques.
Illustrations copyright © 2012 by André Letria.
English translation copyright © 2018 by Chronicle Books LLC.

Library of Congress Cataloging-in-Publication Data available.

ISBN 978-1-4521-5526-5

Manufactured in China.

Design by Jennifer Tolo Pierce.
Typeset in Sabon LT Std and Garage Gothic.

10 9 8 7 6 5 4 3 2 1

Chronicle Books LLC
680 Second Street
San Francisco, California 94107

Chronicle Books—we see things differently. Become part of our
community at www.chroniclekids.com.

If you look at a map of the earth, you will find many seas and oceans, but there is really just one world or global ocean.

Seas are areas of the ocean that are partly enclosed by land.

Landlocked bodies of water, such as the Caspian Sea and the Dead Sea, are often called seas, but these are actually saltwater lakes.

The ocean covers nearly 71 percent of the earth's surface. It is the largest known inhabited space in our universe.

97 percent of the earth's water is found in our oceans. And oceans produce more than half of the oxygen in our atmosphere.

But, really, seawater is colorless. It just looks blue because of how it absorbs the different colored waves in sunlight.

What does sea spray smell like? Does it smell like grilled sardines with salt? Wet sand? And mussels? That is what the sea smells like to me. How would you describe it?

Because the salt in seawater makes the water denser than fresh water, many things that will sink in a lake or a river (or the bathtub) will float in the sea.

The deepest point in the ocean is called the **CHALLENGER DEEP**. It is almost 7 miles (11 kilometres) deep and can be found in the Mariana Trench, in the Pacific Ocean. The first images of the Mariana Trench were taken in 2012 when movie director James Cameron piloted a one-person submersible with 3-D cameras as part of the National Geographic Society's Deepsea Challenge expedition.

On average the ocean is more than 2 miles (3 kilometres) deep.

The underwater ridges that run along the bottom of the oceans form the largest mountain range on earth.

Close your eyes. Could you "catch" your dinner if you were in complete darkness?

A **GIGANTURA** is a deep-sea fish also known as a telescope fish, because its eyes are like powerful telescopes that help it find food in the dark waters where it lives.

1. ARCTIC OCEAN
2. PACIFIC OCEAN
3. ATLANTIC OCEAN
4. BERING SEA
5. GULF OF ALASKA
6. GULF OF MEXICO
7. SARGASSO SEA
8. MEDITERRANEAN SEA
9. BALTIC SEA
10. BLACK SEA
11. CASPIAN SEA
12. DEAD SEA

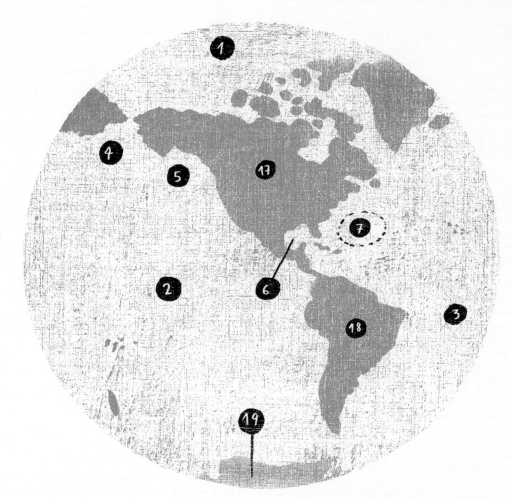

WHAT ARE THE MAJOR OCEANS?

Traditionally, the Atlantic, Pacific, Indian, and Arctic have been known as the four oceans. However, today the Southern, or Antarctic, is usually recognized as the fifth ocean. The Pacific, Atlantic, and Indian are known as the three major oceans.

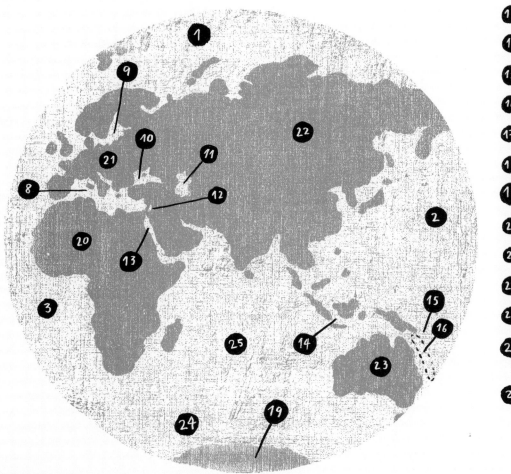

PACIFIC OCEAN

The largest ocean basin is the Pacific. All of the world's continents could fit into the Pacific basin. It covers more than 60 million square miles (155 million square kilometres) and holds more than half of the open water on earth.

The Pacific Ocean was named by Portuguese navigator Ferdinand Magellan in 1520. Pacific means "peaceful."

See the map above? Which sea is nearest to your home?

ATLANTIC OCEAN

The Atlantic Ocean is the second largest ocean basin in the world. Slightly more than half the size of the Pacific Ocean, it covers approximately 20 percent of the earth's surface. The Atlantic Ocean is named after the Greek god Atlas. It plays an important role in controlling the earth's climate.

INDIAN OCEAN

The Indian Ocean covers almost 20 percent of the earth's total surface. It is the warmest ocean in the world, and because of this, it has a much more limited range of wildlife. But it does have many of the world's most important ports and is very rich in minerals and oil. It also features an underwater microcontinent, called the Kerguelen Plateau.

SOUTHERN OCEAN

The Southern Ocean, also known as the Antarctic Ocean, is the fourth largest ocean. In winter over half the Southern Ocean is covered with ice. Beneath the surface of the Antarctic ice, the water temperature can be as cold as 28° Fahrenheit (−2° Celsius).

ARCTIC OCEAN

The Arctic Ocean is the smallest of the world's ocean basins. It is about one and a half times as big as the United States. For most of the year, the Arctic Ocean is almost completely covered with ice. The average thickness of the Arctic ice sheet is about 6 feet (2 metres).

Some fish in cold Antarctic waters have natural antifreeze in their blood so they don't freeze.

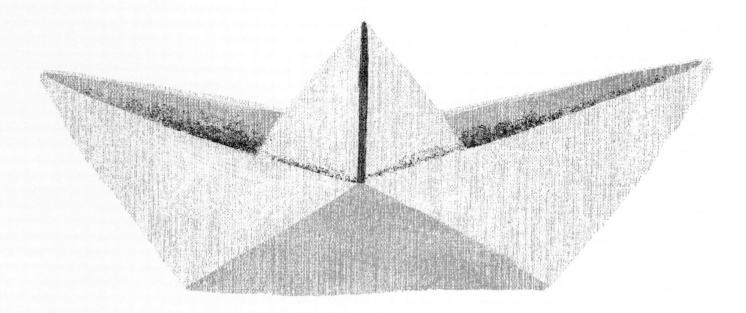

The word "Watercraft" refers to a wide range of vessels that travel on or under water. All boats are watercraft, but not all watercraft are boats.

GALLEON

TUGBOAT

GALLEY

Galleys were ships that were propelled by both sails and rowers.

GALLEON

Galleons were large ships built mostly by the Spanish and Portuguese in the 15th–18th centuries. They were used first as warships and then as trading vessels. The *Flying Dutchman* is a ghost galleon from nautical folklore that is said to be condemned to cross the seas for eternity.

CARRACK

A carrack is a large ship with three to four masts that was developed in 14th- and 15th-century Europe. The name may have come from the Arab word *harraqa*.

TUGBOAT

Tugboats have many jobs but are best known for towing or pushing a vessel to help it dock or leave port.

Get drawing! Sketch your very own boat design.

ICEBREAKER

Icebreakers are ships designed to glide over the top of ice, then break down through it to clear a passageway. The biggest icebreaker in the world is the Russian ship *Artika*. It is 568 feet (173 metres) long, weighs more than 33,000 tons (30,000 tonnes). It can break through ice as thick as 10 feet (3 metres).

SUBMARINE

Submarine means "underwater," and that's exactly where a submarine is designed to go. The first submarine was reportedly built nearly four hundred years ago.

STEAMBOAT

Robert Fulton developed the first functioning steamboat. Steamboats were used in the 19th century in the United States to carry cargo and passengers up and down rivers without having to rely on the currents.

CARAVEL

Caravels were used by Portuguese explorers in the 15th century.

They could range in size from one to four masts and carry a crew of 20 to 60 sailors.

They sometimes had a pair of eyes painted on the bow to help the crew "see the sea ahead"—a tradition that still persists on fishing boats in Portugal.

SEAPLANE

Also known as a hydroplane, a seaplane is an airplane with floats instead of wheels that allow it to take off and land on water. The first seaplane to successfully fly under its own power was built in 1910 by Frenchman Henri Fabre.

STEAMBOAT

CARAVELS

CARAVEL

ANCHOR

Anchors are generally made of steel or iron so that when they are attached to a rope and tossed overboard, they are heavy enough to keep a ship from moving. "To anchor" means to drop the anchor into the water. "To weigh anchor" means to lift it back up.

HATCH

A hatch is an opening that allows cargo and crew to enter and exit the belowdecks area of a ship. It also helps with ventilation and light.

CROW'S NEST

This observation point is at the top of the main (tallest) mast.

BOWSPRIT

The bowsprit is a diagonal spar projecting forward over the bow, or front part of a ship.

FIGUREHEAD

The ancient Egyptians and Greeks mounted decorative carvings of animals at the fronts of their boats. Over time, it became traditional for the figure-head to be a carving of a human.

HULL

The hull is the body of a ship.

BOW

The front part of the hull of a vessel is called the bow (or prow). When a boat moves, water flows on either side of the bow, creating a movement called a *wake*.

STERN

The back end of the hull is called the stern.

KEEL

A keel is a flat blade on the bottom of a sailing boat. It sticks down into the water to prevent the boat from being blown sideways by the wind, and it also helps keep the boat right side up.

PARTS OF SHIP

1. RUDDER
2. STERN
3. SPANKER
4. MIZZENMAST
5. MIZZEN-TOPGALLANT
6. MIZZEN-TOPSAIL
7. MIZZEN COURSE
8. MIZZEN SHROUDS, CHAINS, AND STAYS
9. MAINMAST
10. MAIN TOPGALLANT
11. CROW'S NEST

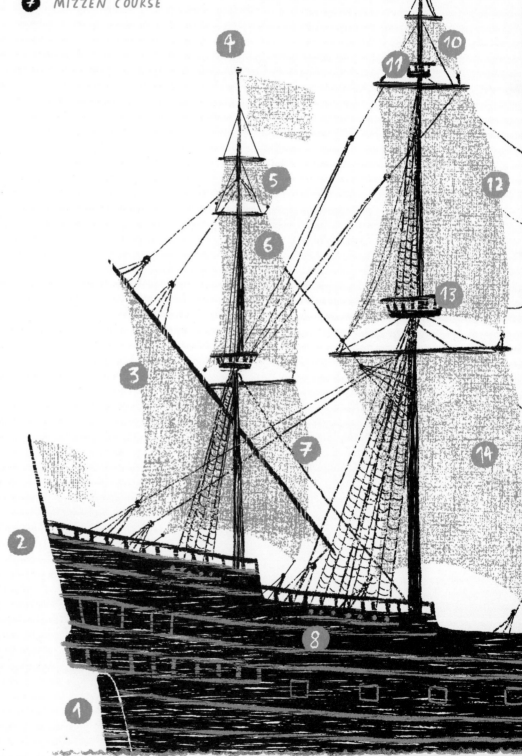

RUDDER

This blade at the stern (back) of a vessel can be moved to change the ship's direction.

HELM

The helm of a boat is used to steer. In a small boat, it is often a tiller, which is a sort of lever that is moved by hand to control the rudder. In a larger ship, a wheel controls the rudder.

MAST

The mast or topmast is a vertical pole attached to the keel in the deck.

PORTHOLE

This round window or opening in the side of a vessel lets in air and light.

WINDWARD

The windward side of a boat is also known as the weather side, because it faces the wind.

STARBOARD SIDE

Before ships had rudders, they were controlled by a steering oar. Most sailors were right handed, so the steering oar was placed on the right side of the boat. Sailors soon began calling the steering side *starboard* (from two Old English words: *stéor*, meaning "steer," and *bord*, meaning "side of a boat"). At night, the right-hand side, starboard, is signaled with a green light.

PORT SIDE

Because it was easier to tie a boat up to a dock on the side opposite the oar, the other side became known as *larboard*, or the "loading side"—but as this was easily confused with starboard, over time it was replaced with *port side*, since this was the side that faced the port. At night the port side is signaled with a red light.

SEEING STARS

For thousands of years, seafarers have used the stars to guide them. Many civilizations have developed stories based on the different constellation shapes in the sky. ORION is one of the best known, since it can be seen in both hemispheres. Son of Poseidon, the sea god, Orion is often depicted as a hunter.

👉 What do you think Orion is carrying?

MERIDIANS are the circles on a map that go from the North Pole to the South Pole. They measure longitude.

PARALLELS are the circles that run perpendicular to the meridians, such as the Equator, which divides the earth in two equal parts (the Northern and the Southern Hemispheres). Parallels measure latitude.

There are 88 named constellations.

👉 **SEE STARS:** Lie down belly-up in the open air on a starry night and try to find Orion and other constellations.

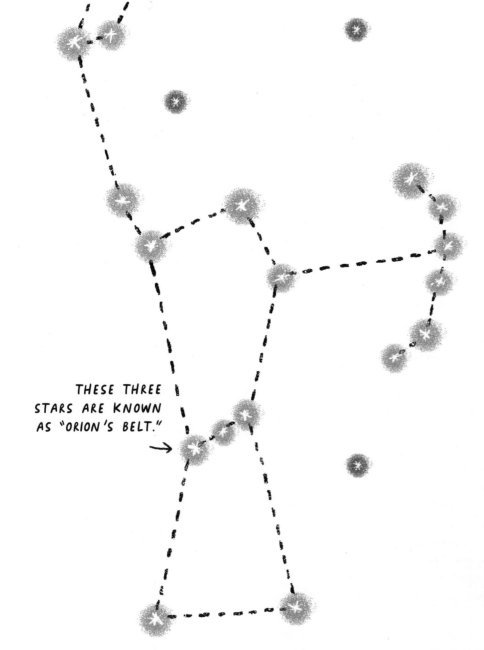

THESE THREE STARS ARE KNOWN AS "ORION'S BELT."

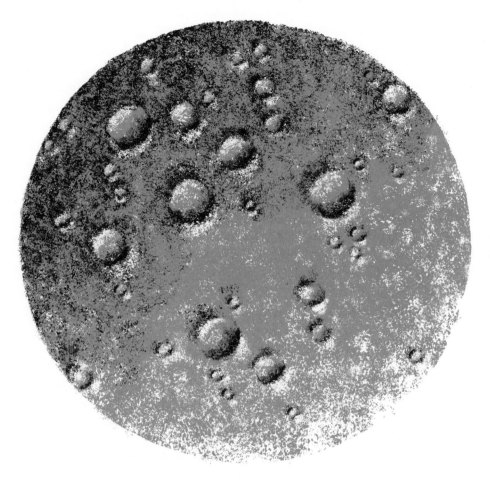

When pointing their telescopes at the moon, the first astronomers saw what looked like lakes, bays, and oceans, including the Sea of Tranquillity. But in reality the moon has no place to swim. These LUNAR MARIA (which comes from the Latin phrase for "lunar seas") are actually volcanic plains.

San Francisco has the longitude and latitude coordinates N 37°46´26, W 122°25´53.

 Use this terminology to schedule dates with your friends.

CHEW ON THIS: After you peel an orange, you will see it looks a bit like a globe. The segments create lines that look like meridians. After reading this entry, go eat an orange. This will prevent scurvy.

MERIDIAN   PARALLEL

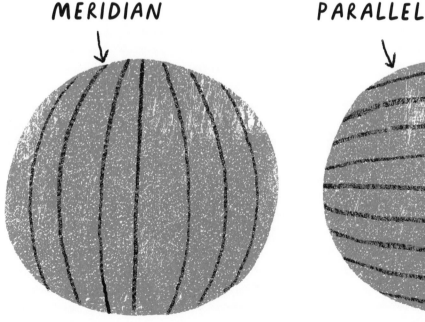
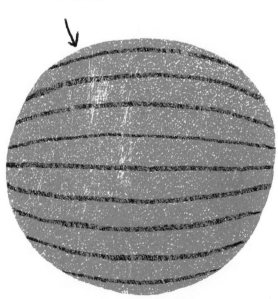

HOW DOES A SHIP NAVIGATE?

While early seafarers relied on the stars to safely find their way, over time many other navigational instruments have been invented.

COMPASS
A modern-day compass uses a magnetized needle that serves as a pointer for determining direction. This needle always points north, to align itself with the magnetic north pole of the earth. Today, GPS (Global Positioning System) has largely taken over the role of the compass.

A **NAUTICAL CHART** shows information on water depth, tides, and hazards such as rocks and shipwrecks.

Whales, dolphins, and bats make sounds that help them detect objects as the sounds bounce back. The French physicist Paul Langevin invented sonar (the name comes from **SOUND NAVIGATION RANGING**), which is based on the same principle. Sonar allows sailors to detect objects under or on the water.

ASTROLABE

The astrolabe is an instrument invented by the ancient Greeks. Astrolabes were first used to measure the position of the stars and to tell time. Eventually, sailors discovered they could be used to navigate at sea. The world's largest collection of astrolabes can be found in the Maritime Museum in Lisbon, Portugal.

SPYGLASS

A spyglass is a handheld telescope. It comes in handy especially when there might be a sea monster preparing an attack or a pirates' ship on the horizon.

SEXTANT

A sextant is a navigation instrument that measures the angles and altitudes of stars. It was developed in the 1700s.

CROSS-STAFF

The cross-staff uses two pieces of wood to measure the altitude of an object above the horizon, or the distance between two objects, such as stars, in the sky. Originally developed in the Middle East, its use can be dated as far back as 400 B.C.

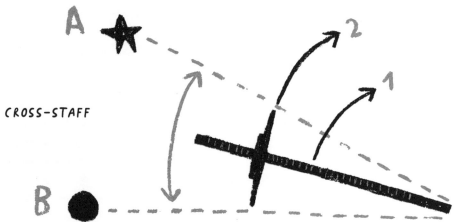

CROSS-STAFF

ACTIVITIES

👉 **HOW TO MAKE A PAPER BOAT**

1. Start with an 8 ½-by-11-inch (21.5-by-28-centimetre) sheet of paper. Fold the paper in half widthwise, top to bottom.

2. Fold the top corners into the center so they meet.

3. Beneath the triangle, you should now have a 1-inch (2.5-cm) flap. Fold the flap up, then turn over and repeat.

4. Pop out the middle and push the bottom corners together to make a square.

5. Fold up the bottom corner of the square, then turn over and repeat to make a triangle.

6. Pop out the middle and push the bottom corners together, as before, to make another square.

7–9. Gently pull apart the upper corners and watch as your square becomes a boat!

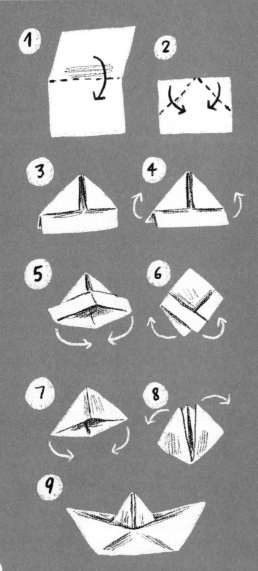

👉 **FIND YOUR WAY**

Earth has a magnetic field that protects it from space radiation. Scientists believe this field is created by electrical currents generated by a core of iron deep inside the planet. Magnetized metals automatically align themselves with this field.

MATERIALS:

Plastic bottle cap or cork
Scissors or other cutting
  instrument
Sewing needle

Bowl or bucket
Strong magnet (most refrigerator
  magnets won't work)

1. If using a plastic bottle cap, have an adult make 2 small notches on opposite sides of the bottle cap with scissors, just big enough for the needle to sit in loosely. If using a cork, have an adult cut a slice of cork approximately ¼ inch (6 mm) thick.

2. Rub the magnet over the needle about 25 times, making sure to always rub in the same direction and to lift the magnet away from the needle after each stroke to reduce the chance of demagnetizing the needle.

3. If using a bottle cap, place the needle in the notches in the cap; if using a cork, tape the needle to one of the flat sides of the cork.

4. Fill a bowl or other container with water.

5. Place the cap or cork in the water, needle-side up. What do you notice?

Because magnetized metals align themselves with earth's magnetic field, once the needle is magnetized and placed in water, it will rotate until it points towards earth's North Magnetic Pole. You can confirm this by comparing your homemade compass to a standard compass or smartphone compass app.

NOTE: Keep the container away from computers and other devices that contain magnets, as they can disrupt the field lines. The needle will slowly lose its magnetic charge over time.

SHIP SHAPE

What makes an object float or sink? It isn't just its weight. (Think about it: ships are very heavy!) Try this to find out.

MATERIALS:

Modeling clay

Glass bowl or other transparent container

1. Shape two balls of modeling clay. Make sure they are the same size. Fill the bowl with water.

2. Flatten one ball of clay with your hands to create a disc. Make sure there are no holes in it, then fold the edges up just a bit.

3. Place both pieces of clay on the surface of the water. What happens?

ALL TIED UP

The figure-eight knot is a good stopper knot to keep a rope from slipping out of a hole.

1. Create a loop with an end.

2. Take the same end and lay it over the rope to make another loop shape.

3. Pass it through the first loop, under and then over, making an 8.

4. Pull both sides to tighten the knot.

DEEP DIVE

MATERIALS:

Plastic bottle

Paper clip

Pen cap (make sure it's the kind without a hole at the top)

1. Fill the bottle with water.

2. Attach the paper clip to the cap.

3. Place the pen cap in the water with the clip facing downwards.

4. Close the bottle. What happens to the pen cap?

5. Squeeze the bottle. What happens now?

6. Stop squeezing. What happens?

A ship is able to float because the weight of the ship is the same as the weight of the water that it displaces. The displacement creates a force that pushes the ship upward, as opposed to gravity, which would pull the ship down. This upward force is called *buoyant force* or *buoyancy*. Unlike a ship, a submarine can control its buoyancy, thus allowing it to dive and surface.

DAILY DISCOVERIES

On his voyage aboard the HMS *Beagle*, Charles Darwin made discoveries that changed the world. Who knows what you will discover if you observe your world closely? All it takes is a notebook, a pencil (or pens or watercolors), and curiosity.

SHIPSHAPE

An orderly life on board a ship requires certain tasks to happen at certain times. For this reason, navy ships established periods of work of four hours, known as *QUARTERS* or *WATCHES*. Every four hours, all sailors change their stations.

Because most sailors couldn't afford to have their own timepieces, time aboard a navy ship was traditionally marked by the ringing of bells. For each watch, one bell was struck after the first half hour has passed, two bells after one hour has passed, and so forth up to eight. Completing a watch with no incidents to report means "eight bells and all is well."

The main events aboard a ship are recorded by the captain in a logbook. Find a blank notebook or make one from pieces of paper. Pretend your home is a ship. Keep a record of what happens all day.

The primary **FOOD** on traditional sailing ships was the biscuit, also known as *sea biscuit* or *hardtack*. These were not the light, fluffy biscuits or cookies we enjoy today, but flat bread that was baked a very long time so it would keep fresh longer.

Long ago, ships were not equipped with tap water or refrigeration, so sailors had to plan their voyages so that they could go ashore to pick up fresh water and food.

SCURVY was a common disease on board ships that travelled long distances. The symptoms include swollen gums, tooth decay, and skin sores. The cause for this illness was lack of vitamin C, which comes from fresh fruits and vegetables. From the 18th century on, food on board ships included citrus, which made the illness disappear.

SEASICKNESS, or motion sickness, is caused when one part of your balance-sensing system senses that your body is moving, but other parts don't. For example, if you are in the cabin of a moving ship, your inner ear may sense the motion of waves, but your eyes don't see any movement.

BEARDS

When we think of explorers and pirates, both real and imaginary, we almost always envision them with a beard. In fact, one of the most notorious pirates was Edward Teach, known as Blackbeard.

☞ Ask your parents to make copies of some family photos for you. Then draw beards on all your relatives!

There are no traffic signs on the high sea, but there is the INTERNATIONAL CODE OF SIGNALS. Messages can be sent using signal lamps, flags printed with special symbols, or semaphore, a system that uses arm movements that symbolize the letters of the alphabet.

Try using this method to speak with your family.

The **WHITE FLAG** is one of the international symbols for peace. During a battle, hoisting this flag means surrender to the enemy.

TO BE OR KNOT TO BE?

Every sailor knows how to tie knots. Here are some of the most common.

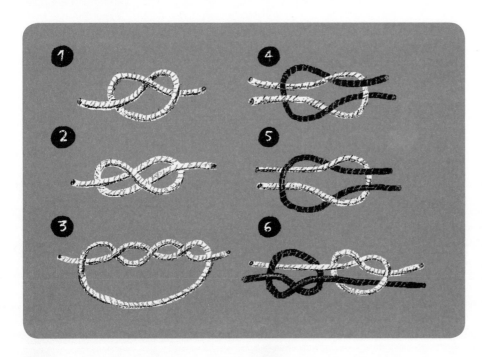

1 OVERHAND KNOT		**4** GRANNY KNOT	
2 FIGURE-EIGHT KNOT		**5** SQUARE KNOT	
3 DOUBLE OVERHEAD KNOT		**6** FISHERMAN'S KNOT	

A ship's **CREW** is often from all over the world. Because confusion can lead to dangerous situations, in 1983 a new system of communication called Seaspeak was created.

A good **PARTY** has to have balloons and clowns, right? Wrong! It needs champagne bottles. A ship is traditionally launched by breaking a bottle of champagne against the hull. According to the superstition, it is a bad omen if the bottle does not break.

When using Seaspeak on a ship's radio, the number of words is limited to ensure that messages are clear. And each interaction is preceded by one of eight words, called message markers: Advice, Answer, Information, Instruction, Intention, Question, Request, and Warning. Try using this method to speak with your family.

There are **KNOTS** you tie and knots you travel. The knots sailors tie all have a specific function on board the ship. For example, the figure-eight knot is used to prevent a rope or line from getting loose, and the fisherman's knot is used to mend cables.

A different kind of knot is used to measure speed. One knot equals a nautical mile (2,025 yards or 1,852 metres) per hour. The term comes from the 17th century, when sailors measured how fast their ships were traveling by using a rope with evenly spaced knots, called a "common log." This was dropped into the water and allowed to run out for a certain amount of time. When the rope was pulled back in, the number of knots on the rope that had gone into the water was counted to determine the ship's speed.

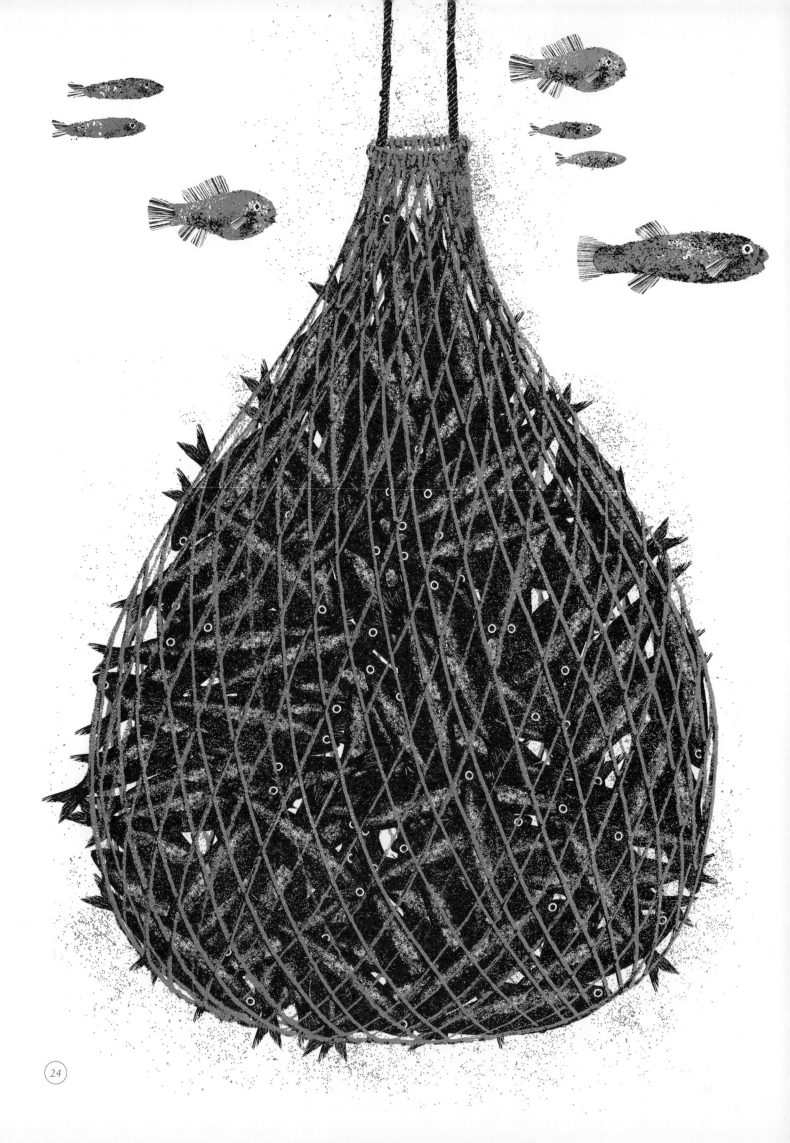

People all around the world depend on the ocean for their food. Each year more than 75 million tons (68 million tonnes) of fish are caught in the ocean. Many species of fish, including tuna, salmon, and cod, are endangered by overfishing.

Species of **COD** can be found in both the Atlantic and Pacific Oceans, but cod is a particularly important part of traditional cultures in Portugal and New England. Long before refrigeration was invented, fisherman caught cod and salted it to preserve it for the coming months. In the 19th century, codfish weighing up to 200 pounds (90 kilograms) used to be caught. Nowadays, due to overfishing, a 40-pound (18-kilogram) cod is considered a giant.

☞ Although North Atlantic cod was recently removed from the endangered list, visit websites like www.seafoodwatch.org to learn what kinds of cod are the best choice.

HUMANS have fished for thousands and thousands of years. Mounds of shells, some from prehistoric times, have been found along coasts around the world, showing that mollusks were among our earliest foods.

Once humans learned to catch fish in traps and nets, they were able to travel off the shore and out to sea to catch fish in deeper waters.

Early humans were only able to catch as much fish as they could use right away. With the invention of food preservation techniques such as drying, smoking, and salting, it was possible to store larger amounts.

Today, **COMMERCIAL FISHERMEN** around the world harvest a wide variety of species. However, herring, cod, anchovy, tuna, flounder, squid, shrimp, and salmon make up the majority of fish sold.

👉 ICEBERG IN THE KITCHEN

MATERIALS:

Paper or plastic cup	Tub, bowl, or other large container
Water	(it should be taller than the cup)

1. Fill the cup with water and place it in the freezer.

2. When the water has frozen, remove the ice from the cup.

3. Fill the large container with water.

4. Put the ice in the water. What do you notice?

ICEBERG IN THE KITCHEN

👉 SINK OR SWIM

Why do some objects float in water and others sink? Does it have to do with weight? Ships are certainly heavy. So perhaps there is another factor involved. Here is an *egg*-cellent way to find out.

MATERIALS

2 glasses (the same size)	Salt
Measuring cup	Spoon
Water	2 eggs, at room temperature

1. Fill each glass with 1 cup (240 ml) water.

2. Add 4 tbsp salt to one of the glasses and stir until it is fully dissolved. (This may take some time.)

3. Use the spoon to carefully place an egg into each glass. What happens? Why do you think this is?

Because an egg is denser than plain tap water, the egg in plain water sinks. But, if you add enough salt to the water, the egg will float. So whether an object will float has to do with its relative density. If an object is less dense than the water around it, it floats. And since salt water is denser than freshwater, things float more easily in salty bodies of water. Do you think an egg would float in seawater?

BONUS ACTIVITY: You can determine just how salty the water needs to be to allow an egg to be buoyant, by varying the ratio of salt to water. Start with very salty water. And then add a bit more water, and a bit more, until the egg sinks.

👉 OCEAN IN A BOTTLE

Now you can have the power of Neptune!

MATERIALS:

Plastic bottle with cap	Water
Cooking oil	Food coloring

1. Fill the bottle one-quarter of the way full with oil.

2. Add water until the bottle is half full.

3. Add a few drops of food coloring.

4. Close the bottle and hold it horizontally.

5. Shake the bottle from side to side to create waves. What do you notice?

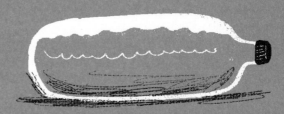

👉 LOG ON

Be captain of your own life. Create a journal to note what you do each day.

CALDEIRADA (PORTUGUESE FISH STEW)

Prep time: 30 minutes / Cooking time: 1 hour / Serves 6

Nothing is as tasty as a plate of grilled fish or a bowl of fish stew. From the Bouillabaisse of France to San Francisco's Cioppino, most fishing communities have a local recipe for fish stew to use up leftovers from the day's catch. This delicious version is from Portugal.

INGREDIENTS

1/4 cup (60 millilitres) olive oil

8 ounces (225 grams) linguica, chorizo, or other spicy sausage, cut into 1/2-inch (12-millimetre) rounds

2 medium onions, thinly sliced

4 garlic cloves, minced

1 green bell pepper, sliced into strips

2 tablespoons chopped flat-leaf parsley, plus more for garnish

2 Yukon Gold potatoes, peeled and diced

Pinch of saffron (or fennel seed)

1 bay leaf

Two 14.5-ounce (410-grams) cans of diced tomatoes, with juice

1/4 cup (60 grams) tomato paste (optional)

1 tablespoon anchovy paste (optional)

1/4 cup (60 millilitres) dry white wine

1/2 cup (120 millilitres) water

1 pound (450 grams) white fish, such as sea bass, monkfish, hake, or haddock

8 ounces (225 grams) large prawns

1 dozen clams

1 dozen mussels

8 ounces (225 grams) squid (optional)

Freshly ground black pepper

Crusty bread for serving

1. In a large stockpot, heat the olive oil over medium heat. Add the suasage and cook, stirring often, until it releases its fat and begins to brown.

2. Add the onion, garlic, and green bell pepper. Cook uncovered for about 10 minutes.

3. Cover, turn the heat to low, and cook for another 15 minutes, stirring occasionally.

4. Add the parsley, potatoes, saffron, bay leaf, diced tomatoes, tomato paste (if using), anchovy paste (if using), wine, and water. Cover and simmer for 10 minutes.

5. Add the fish, prawns, clams, mussels, and squid (if using) in layers. Don't stir; you want the fish to cook in the broth.

6. Season with black pepper. Cover and cook for about 10—15 minutes, or until the fish is cooked through and the mussels and clams have opened. (Discard any that don't open.)

7. Ladle the stew gently into bowls, topping with a bit of chopped parsley, and serve with bread.

SCHOOL OF FISH

Scientists estimate that there are about twenty-two thousand species of fish in the ocean. **Here are the names of some of them.**

BLOWFISH	LIONFISH
COFFINFISH	DOGFISH
BOXFISH	LANTERN SHARK
BELTFISH	GHOST SHARK
BOARFISH	HAMMERHEAD SHARK
ANGLERFISH	WHALE SHARK
SUNFISH	BASKING SHARK
CLOWNFISH	GOBLIN SHARK

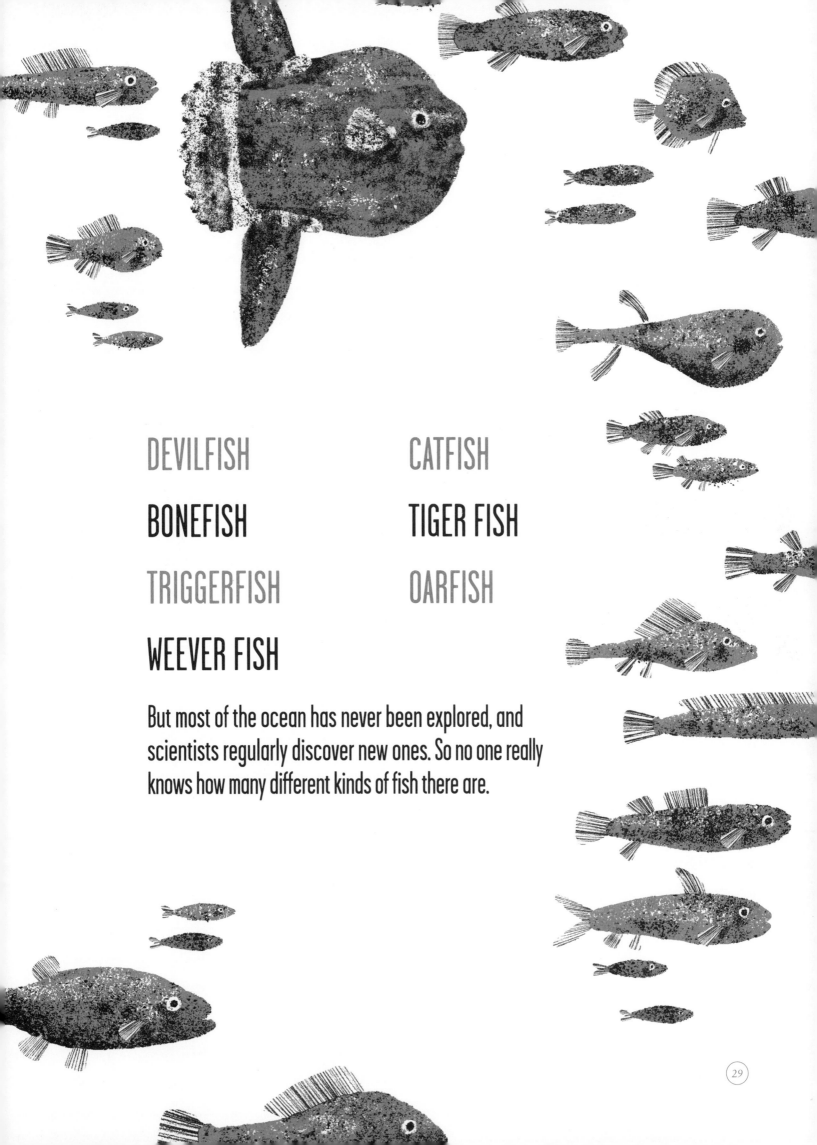

DEVILFISH

CATFISH

BONEFISH

TIGER FISH

TRIGGERFISH

OARFISH

WEEVER FISH

But most of the ocean has never been explored, and scientists regularly discover new ones. So no one really knows how many different kinds of fish there are.

The CENSUS OF MARINE LIFE was an international project that recorded the diversity of life in the ocean. For ten years, thousands of scientists from around the world created millions of records describing more than 1,200 new marine species. Thousands more await formal descriptions. The information will serve as a record when future researchers measure changes to ocean habitats.

BLUE WHALE

The largest animal to ever live on earth is the blue whale. It can reach lengths of 98 feet (30 metres), about the height of an eleven-story building, and can weigh more than 150 tons (136 tonnes). Its heart is the size of a golf cart.

KRILL

Krill are small crustaceans similar to shrimps that feed on plankton, tiny particles that hover in the sea. Krill is really important in the food chain, being part of the diet of many whales, penguins, seals, and small fish.

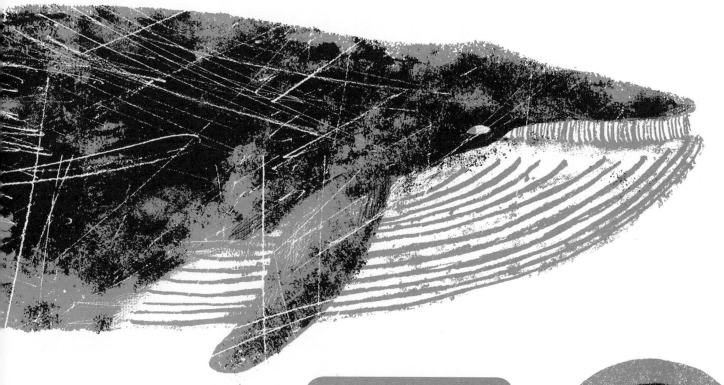

FIN

Many aquatic animals have fins that allow them to balance and move about. Fish usually have a dorsal fin, an anal fin, a caudal (or tail) fin, two pelvic fins and, behind their gills, two pectoral fins.

PINNIPEDS

Sea lions, seals, and walrus are *pinnipeds*, meaning "fin-footed" or "flipper-footed."

☞ Can you guess which is which? **HINT:** Seals do not have visible ears and walrus have tusks.

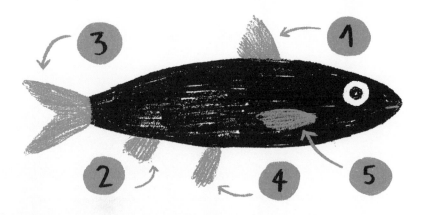

1 DORSAL FIN

2 ANAL FIN

3 CAUDAL (OR TAIL) FIN

4 PELVIC FIN

5 PECTORAL FIN

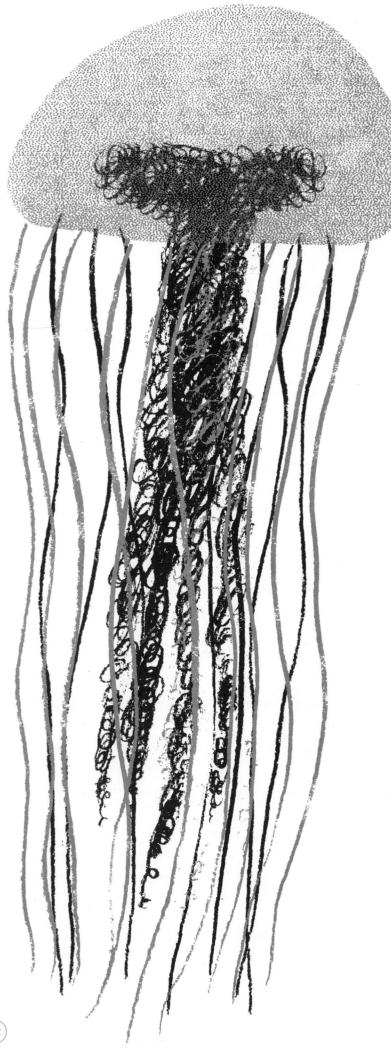

JELLYFISH
Elegant, mysterious, and with a deadly sting, a jellyfish out of the water becomes a much less fascinating blob. This is because jellyfish are about 95 percent water.

SEA STAR
There are about two thousand different species of sea star. A sunflower sea star can have more than twenty arms, with an arm span of more than 3 feet (1 metre).

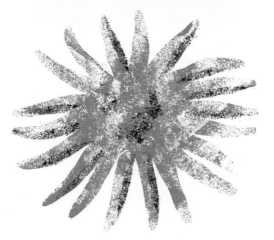

Coral colonies are called **REEFS**, the largest of which is the Great Barrier Reef, on Australia's coast. It is considered the largest structure on earth made by living organisms. It is more than 1,243 miles (2,300 kilometres) long. It can even be seen from space.

Although coral reefs make up less than 1 percent of the ocean floor, it is estimated that more than one million marine species make their homes in or around them.

BRAIN CORAL doesn't have a brain, but many scientists consider it one of the most advanced species of coral. The foundations of many reefs are formed by brain coral.

Carry a notebook wherever you go. Draw what you see around you—it could be a sea star, a bird … or your dog.

Nearly **60 percent of the world's remaining reefs are at risk of being lost** in the next three decades, due to coastal development, destructive fishing practices, pollution, tourism, and global warming.

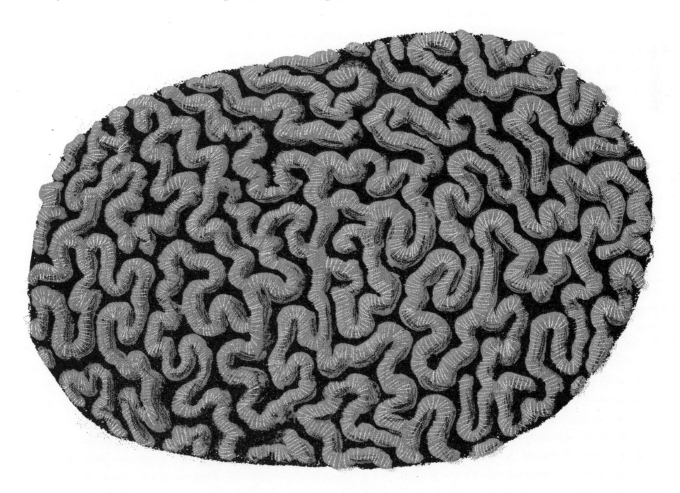

TALES FROM THE DEEP

SUPERSTITIONS

Because sailing was so dangerous, sailors developed many superstitions. It was considered bad luck to shave a beard, sing, whistle into the wind, or have a cargo of bananas aboard.

MERMAIDS

Mermaids have been part of mythology since humans first began telling stories. The ancient Greek poet Homer wrote about them in *The Odyssey*. In the ancient Far East, mermaids were believed to be married to sea dragons, and were thought to serve as messengers between the dragons and the emperors on land. The aboriginal people of Australia call mermaids *yawkyawks*.

KRAKEN

The kraken is a mythological creature that originated in the imaginations of mariners who sailed the north seas. It may have been inspired by the giant squid, a deep-sea creature rarely seen by humans.

NEPTUNE

Son of Saturn, brother of Jupiter and Pluto, Neptune was the Roman god of the seas. He is usually depicted with a trident in his hand and often in a shell-shaped carriage pulled by seahorses. Like most Roman gods, Neptune is a remake of a Greek god, in this case the god Poseidon.

SOLEMN PRESENTATION: In the Greek and Roman times it was common that people introduced themselves with the name of their parents. Introduce yourself like that, solemnly.

SAFE HARBOR

LIGHTHOUSES

Lighthouses are designed to help ships navigate safely through the rocky shoals along a coast. In ancient times lighthouses were lit with fires or whale oil lamps. Later, gas and finally electricity were used to power the signal beacons.

BUOYS

Buoys are frequently used to mark hazards, though there are many kinds of buoys. Often they are brightly colored or have lights so they are more easily spotted.

CURRENTS

The water in the ocean moves constantly. Cold, deep currents run from the poles toward the Equator, while warm, shallow currents are driven the opposite way. The temperature of the water, the amount of salt in the water, and the earth's rotation all influence currents, which in turn can affect our weather.

After a **SQUALL** (a violent marine thunderstorm) comes the calm. This is a time for sailors to take a nap!

Clouds can tell a sailor what type of weather is coming. Cirrus clouds are very high up in the sky and are often at the front of a storm. Cumulus clouds are lower and forecast good weather. Draw what you see in the clouds.

WAVES

The ocean is never still. Its movement can be seen in the endless waves that lap the shore. Some waves are caused by the gravitational pull of the moon, others by underwater earthquakes. Most are caused by the wind. However, what we see as moving water is really ENERGY that is traveling across the ocean. If there is nothing in its way, a wave can travel all the way across an ocean basin. The saying "making waves" means to cause trouble, but don't say that to a surfer!

THERE ARE MANY DIFFERENT KINDS OF WAVES, INCLUDING— WIND WAVES, OCEAN SWELLS, TIDAL WAVES, SPILLING BREAKERS, AND PLUNGING BREAKERS.

Waves can also be caused by underwater earthquakes, landslides, or volcanic eruptions. These very long waves are called *TSUNAMIS* and can travel as fast as a jet plane. At sea, they are hard to see because sometimes they're no more than 1 foot (30 centimetres) high. As they come toward the shore, they often reach 10 feet (3 metres) tall, but the tallest tsunami wave on record was 100 feet (30 metres) high!

SINCE THE EARLIEST OF TIMES, HUMANS HAVE TAKEN TO THE SEAS TO EXPLORE.

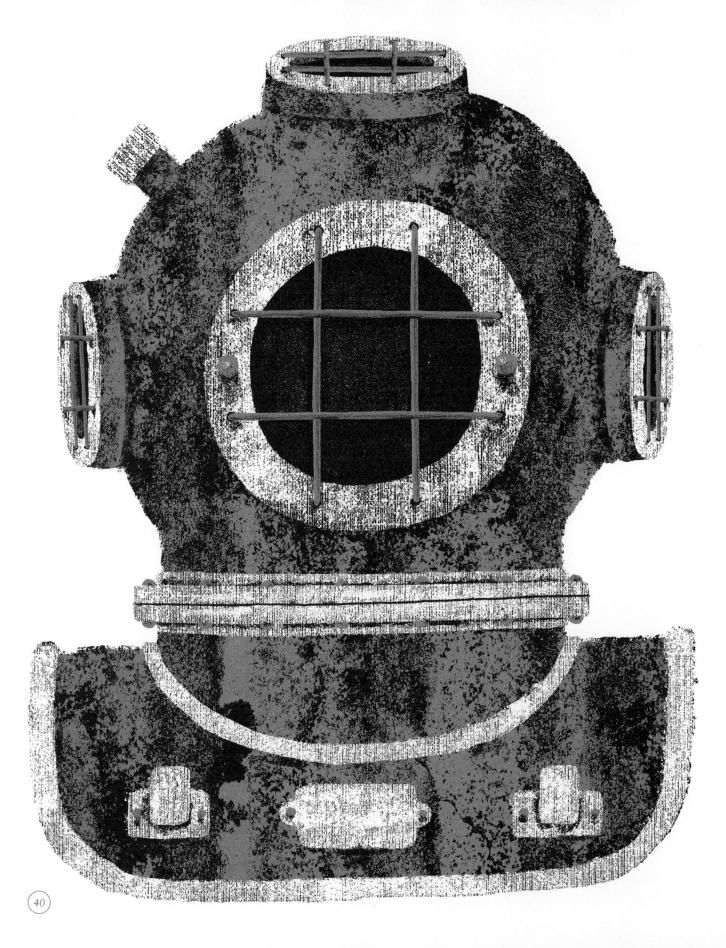

FERDINAND MAGELLAN
Believed to have been the first sailor to circumnavigate (sail entirely around) the earth.

LEIF ERIKSON
Around 500 years before Columbus, a Viking was the first European to set foot on what is now known as North America.

HEZHENG
One of the earliest Chinese explorers. He traveled throughout Asia and to Africa and the Middle East.

IBN BATTUTA
A famous medieval Muslim explorer. Born in northern Africa, he traveled by both land and boat across Africa and the Middle East.

CHARLES DARWIN
One of the most important biologists and naturalists to have lived. Famous for his theory of evolution, described in his book *On the Origin of the Species* (published in 1859), he developed many of his scientific theories while exploring the Galapagos Islands on the ship HMS *Beagle*.

JACQUES COUSTEAU
The science that studies oceans is called oceanography. Jacques Cousteau was one of the world's most notable oceanographers. He was the co-inventor of the Aqua-Lung— what we now call a scuba tank— and millions of people around the world explored the seas from home by watching the many documentary films he made.

SCUBA was originally an acronym, **S.C.U.B.A.,** for "self-contained underwater breathing apparatus."

While humans had been experimenting with ideas for underwater diving for centuries, it wasn't until the beginning of the nineteenth century that the invention of diving helmets made it possible to breathe underwater. Long hoses attached these brass helmets to air pumps onboard nearby boats.

SATELLITES orbiting the earth can provide us with information about the entire global ocean in a few days or weeks. It would take ships weeks or months to make the trip around the earth.

TIP OF THE ICEBERG

Icebergs are large floating blocks of ice that drift in the oceans and create a great risk for ships. The *TITANIC*, the biggest transatlantic ship of its time, sank in less than three hours because of an iceberg.

As much as 90 percent of an iceberg is hidden underwater, which explains the expression **"THE TIP OF THE ICEBERG,"** referring to something that has more to be revealed.

The Arctic produces more than thirty thousand icebergs each year. None of them will fit in your freezer.

ICEBERGS ARE MONITORED WORLDWIDE BY THE U.S. NATIONAL ICE CENTER

ICEBERG

To be classified as an iceberg, the ice must be taller than 16 feet (4.8 metres) above sea level, at least 98 feet (30 metres) thick, and cover an area of at least 5,382 square feet (500 square metres).

Icebergs are also classified by shape, most commonly being either tabular or nontabular. Tabular icebergs have steep sides and a flat top. Nontabular icebergs have different shapes, with domes and spires.

There are also smaller pieces of ice known as *bergy bits* and *growlers*, which can originate from glaciers or shelf ice or can occur as a result of a large iceberg that has broken apart.

Most icebergs look white, but they can also be blue and green. When an iceberg is underwater, the compressed ice absorbs longer wavelengths of color, such as red and yellow, allowing us to see just the colors of shorter wavelengths, like green and blue. Also, algae often grow on the underwater portions of icebergs, creating green stripes in the ice.

PERIL AT SEA

There are many reasons ships sink. Sometimes they are poorly built. Sometimes even the best built ships are destroyed in storms. In wartime, a ship may be purposely sunk by another ship. And sometimes ships accidentally collide with one another.

On average more than **FORTY THOUSAND BARRELS OF OIL A YEAR** is accidentally spilled from ships.

The worst oil tanker spill in history happened when the supertanker *Atlantic Empress* collided with another supertanker in the Caribbean Sea. The accident cost the lives of 26 crew members and caused 88.3 million gallons (334 million litres) of oil to spill into the ocean.

Sometimes a sunken ship can't be found. But even if we know exactly where a sunken ship lies, it can be very hard (or impossible) to recover it.

Over the course of history, many lives have been lost in shipwrecks. Some sunken ships, like the *Flying Dutchman*, have inspired ghostly legends. It is said that the ship's captain ran into a storm off the Cape of Good Hope in Africa. He swore that he would "spite God's wrath" by sailing into the storm, but the ship, along with its entire crew, sank. Legend has it that as punishment, the captain and his ghostly crew were to sail for eternity, waiting to be forgiven.

In some cases, a sunken ship serves as the start of a new reef, becoming a new habitat for sea creatures and protecting biodiversity.

Christopher Columbus's ships— the *Niña*, the *Pinta*, and the *Santa Maria*—sailed to the New World, but only two returned to Spain. The sailor in charge of steering the *Santa Maria* handed the wheel over to a cabin boy, who ran the vessel onto a coral reef near Haiti. The crew was saved, but the ship sank, and no one knows its exact location.

In 1914, **ERNEST SHACKLETON** attempted to make the first land crossing of Antarctica. But before he reached his destination, his ship, the ***ENDURANCE***, became trapped in heavy pack ice. Though Shackleton and his crew escaped by traveling 800 dangerous miles (1,300 kilometres) in a lifeboat, the *Endurance* was lost. It is believed that the ship is 10,000 feet (3,000 metres) underwater, covered by a 5-foot (1.5-metre) layer of ice.

The GREAT PACIFIC GARBAGE PATCH is a collection of marine debris in the Pacific Ocean. No one really knows how big it is, but it is believed to contain millions of pieces. Most of the debris is plastic, which is not biodegradable. When the plastic breaks up into tiny pieces, it can create a danger for many marine animals.

MORE TALES FROM THE DEEP

MOBY-DICK by Herman Melville was published in 1851. It tells the story of Ahab, a captain blinded by hate for a white whale. The book's opening—"Call me Ishmael"—is one of the most famous literary lines in the world. Although Moby-Dick was not a real whale, the novel was inspired by real-life events.

The epic Greek poem, ***THE ODYSSEY***, is almost 3000 years old. It tells the story of Odysseus's long journey home from war and is considered one of the most important works of western literature. Experts can't agree on whether or not the places Odysseus visits are real or imaginary.

THE LITTLE MERMAID by Danish author Hans Christian Andersen was first published in 1837. It is told around the word and has been made into an opera and ballet as well as movies. A bronze statue of the little mermaid can be found perched on a rock along the harbor of Copenhagen in Denmark.

A tale from the Zulu people of South Africa says that the sounds we hear when we hold a seashell to our ear is the **GIFT OF STORIES** from the King and Queen of the Sea.

The *NAUTILUS* is an imaginary submarine commanded by Captain Nemo, that appears in the book *TWENTY THOUSAND LEAGUES UNDER THE SEA*, written by Jules Verne. It was inspired by the real-life submarine *NAUTILUS*, which was created in 1800 by American inventor Robert Fulton, for Napoleon Bonaparte.

A nautilus is also a mollusk with a spiral-shaped shell that has many compartments. The animal lives in the shell's largest chamber, while the other chambers act as ballast tanks, similar to those in a submarine.

KON-TIKI

In 1947, Norwegian writer and explorer Thor Heyerdahl traveled by raft across the Pacific Ocean from South America to Polynesia to show how humans may have traveled long ago. His book about the journey, *Kon-Tiki: Across the Pacific in a Raft*, became a best-seller and a movie. The raft itself is on display in a museum in Oslo, Norway.

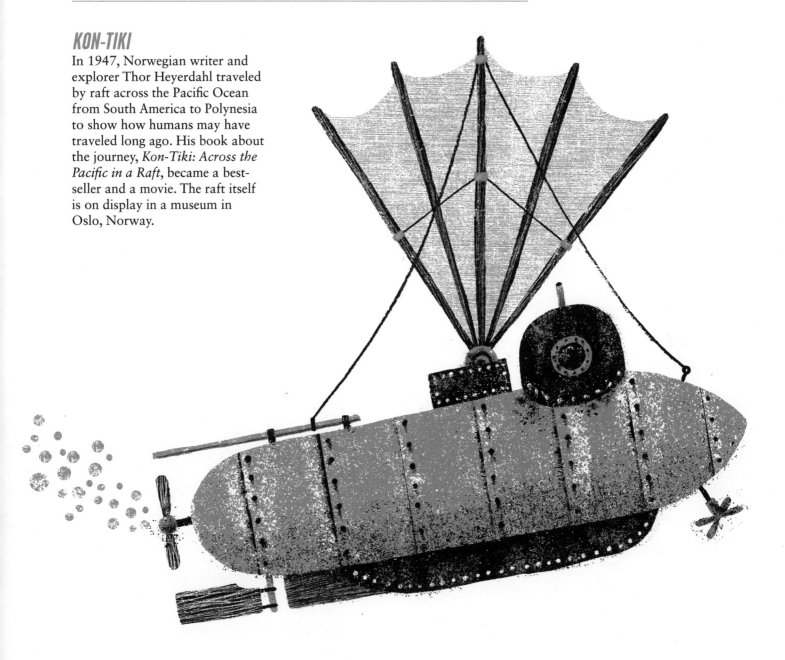

Of the more than eight million species of animals on earth, it is estimated that **MORE THAN TWO MILLION** live in the oceans.

The ocean is the lifeblood of the earth, driving weather, regulating temperature, and ultimately supporting all living organisms. Throughout history, the ocean has been a vital source of sustenance, transport, commerce, growth, and inspiration. Yet for all of our reliance on the ocean, so far we have explored less than 5 percent of the ocean. 95 PERCENT OF THIS REALM REMAINS UNSEEN BY HUMAN EYES.

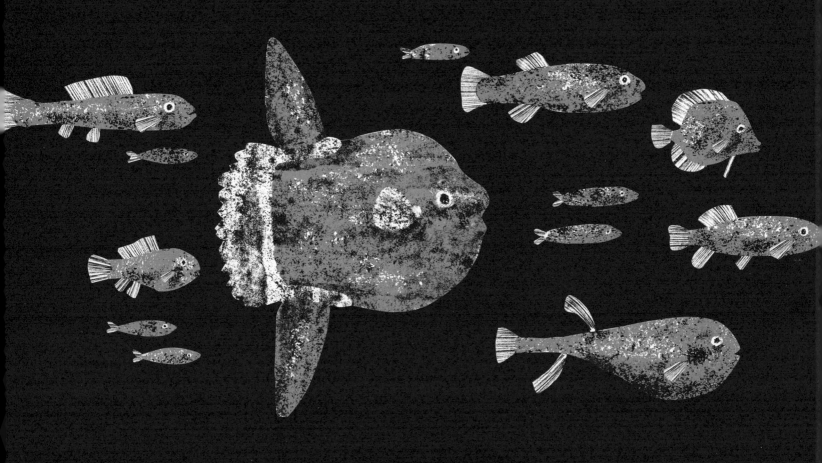

THE SEA, ONCE IT CASTS ITS SPELL, HOLDS ONE IN ITS NET OF WONDER FOREVER. —JACQUES COUSTEAU

ATLANTIC OCEAN • DAVIS STRAIT • LABRADOR SEA • GUL
MASSACHUSETTS BAY • NANTUCKET SOUND • BUZZARDS B
BAY • CHESAPEAKE BAY • GULF OF MEXICO • BAY OF CAMPE
• MOSQUITO GULF • GULF OF VENEZUELA • GULF OF PARIA •
SEA • WADDEN SEA • BALTIC SEA • ARCHIPELAGO SEA • GULF
• SEA OF ÅLAND • ENGLISH CHANNEL • IRISH SEA • CELTIC
SEA • ADRIATIC SEA • AEGEAN SEA • SEA OF CRETE • THRA
IONIAN SEA • LEVANTINE SEA • LIBYAN SEA • LIGURIAN SEA
OF MARMARA • BLACK SEA • SEA OF AZOV • GULF OF GUINE
SIBERIAN SEA • LAPTEV SEA • KARA SEA • BARENTS SEA •
BAFFIN BAY • NORTHWEST PASSAGE • PRINCE GUSTAV ADO
JAMES BAY • BEAUFORT SEA • SOUTHERN OCEAN • AMUNDSE
SEA • COSMONAUTS SEA • DAVIS SEA • DUMONT D'URVILLE S
VINCENT • KING HAAKON VII SEA • LAZAREV SEA • MAWSON
SEA • SPENCER GULF • WEDDELL SEA • INDIAN OCEAN • AN
• GULF OF OMAN • LACCADIVE SEA • MOZAMBIQUE CHANNEL
ARAFURA SEA • BALI SEA • BANDA SEA • BERING SEA • BISM
SEA • CERAM SEA • CHILEAN SEA • SEA OF CHILOÉ • CORA
GULF OF CALIFORNIA • GULF OF CARPENTARIA • GULF OF TH
GRAU • MOLUCCA SEA • PHILIPPINE SEA • SALISH SEA •
SIBUYAN SEA • SOLOMON SEA • SOUTH CHINA SEA • SULU SE